Crafty Little Fingers

Lesley Mason

Illustrated by Bettina Paterson

Photographed by Lucy Tizard

MACDONALD YOUNG BOOKS

For Mum and Dad

This book was created for Macdonald Young Books by Wendy Knowles
Design, layout and typesetting: Roger Kohn Designs

First published in 1996 by Macdonald Young Books

Text, design and illustrations © Macdonald Young Books 1996
Illustrations © Bettina Paterson 1996

Macdonald Young Books
61 Western Road
Hove
East Sussex BN3 1JD

Printed and bound by Edições ASA, Portugal

A catalogue record for this book is available from the British Library

ISBN 0 7500 1885 2
1886 0 (pb)

*Pages 30–32: the Author and Publishers are grateful to 'Never, Never Land',
Muswell Hill, for the loan of dolls house furniture and accessories.*

For your safety

Have fun with the projects in *Crafty Little Fingers* –
but remember that an adult should
always be nearby when you are using
sharp tools such as scissors or needles
and whenever you see this symbol
... it means that adult help is essential at that point.
If you follow these simple rules it will help keep you safe:

❀ when painting or glueing, wear an overall or old shirt to protect
your clothes from paint or glue splashes

❀ always cover any surfaces that you are working on

❀ be careful to keep glue away from your eyes, nose and mouth

❀ if you have long hair tie it back

❀ always ask an adult to help you if you need to use very sharp
scissors or any sharp tools

❀ remember to wash your paintbrushes thoroughly after you
have finished painting.

Contents

Glitterstone space monsters

Make your own weird and wonderful space monsters from pebbles and stones, complete with goggly eyes and antennae, and a spaceship.

You will need

- Small pebbles and stones
- Acrylic paints and brush
- Fine glitter
- PVA glue
- Safety scissors
- Thick thread
- Clear multi-purpose craft glue

For the spaceship

- 3 small foil pie dishes
- Fine fuse wire for ladder and antennae
- Silver or invisible tape
- Frayed silver ribbon and modelling clay or plasticine

Time to take off

4

What to do

1 **Collect your pebbles and stones in a container**
Give them a wash.

2 **Choose the colours for your monsters' skins**
Paint the pebbles and stones.

3 **When the paint is dry**
Brush a layer of PVA glue on them, then sprinkle fine glitter over their backs.

4 **Now for their eyes!**
First paint 2 white dots, then, when they are dry, 2 black dots in the middle of the white.

5 **Give your monsters feelers**
Take a piece of thick thread about 5 cm long, dip both ends in paint, leave to dry, then stick the thread on to your glitter-stone monster with clear glue.

6 **Make them a spaceship**
Paint foil dishes. Tape 2 together as the 'ship'. Cut and shape the third to be the spaceship 'launcher'. Glue this on to your spaceship with clear glue.

You could decorate your spaceship with radar antennae and a ladder or make some moon landscape trees out of frayed silver ribbon and plasticine.

Minibeasts from beans and seeds

Create your own amazing collection of minibeasts. Keep them in a matchbox or make them a habitat.

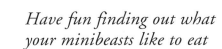

Have fun finding out what your minibeasts like to eat

6

Ladybirds – What to do

1 Select your beans
Paint 1 side of each bean black. Then leave to dry.

2 Turn your beans over
Paint the other side red and leave it to dry.

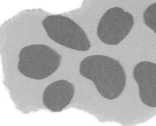

3 Now for the heads and spots!
With a very little black paint on your brush, give your ladybirds their heads and spots.

4 Eyes next
Dip your brush in the white paint and add 2 tiny white dots to make the eyes.

5 Brush PVA glue all over the leaves and let them dry
The glue will preserve the colour of the leaves and help them to keep their shape.

6 Arrange your ladybirds on the leaves.
Then glue them in place with clear glue.

You can make other minibeasts in the same way. Paint your bean or seed first to make your minibeast's head and body. Then, using clear glue, stick on small pieces of thick thread dipped in PVA glue for legs and antennae. Don't forget, spiders have 8 legs!

Dress up eggs – as animals!

Decide if your egg animals need to stand upright or not, on the bottle top

For a 'Bugs Bunny' rabbit, give him a triangle-shaped nose, 2 teeth and a bow tie, and stand him upright

All you need to make these animal friends is a box of large eggs, some paints and some small scraps of coloured felt, yarn and cotton wool.

You will need

* Box of eggs (for blowing) or hard-boiled eggs
* Darning needle
* Small bowl
* Acrylic paints
* Paintbrush
* Small scraps of coloured felt; try, **for chick:** beak (orange), wings (yellow), feet (yellow or orange), eyes (black or white – or both) **for sheep:** face (black), ears (white or black), eyes (white or another colour), nose (pink, brown or white) **for rabbit:** face (white/brown or light brown), ears (pink/brown or brown/light brown), nose (pink or brown), eyes (black or brown/white) **for mouse:** ears (pink or pink/grey), nose (black or pink), eyes (black)
* Small cotton wool balls (for sheep's coat, rabbit's tail)
* Pipecleaner (for sheep's tail)
* Wool or yarn (for mouse's tail, sheep and rabbit's mouths)
* Short lengths of cotton thread (for rabbit's and mouse's whiskers)
* Clear craft glue and glue brush
* Bottle tops (to stand your animals on)
* Safety scissors

What to do

1. Make a hole in the pointed end of your egg with the needle
Then make a bigger hole at the other end.

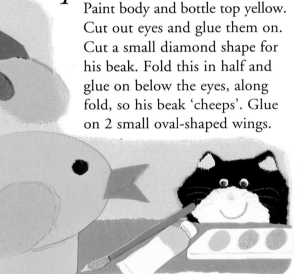

2. Now empty your egg
Hold it over a bowl. Blow hard through the small top hole of the egg so that all the egg comes out of the big hole and into the bowl. Rinse egg clean under a tap and stand it to drain and dry before painting.

3. Mouse
Paint body and bottle top grey. Cut out ears, nose and eyes and glue them on. Glue on whiskers and a tail. You can glue the wool tail into the hole.

4. Chick
Paint body and bottle top yellow. Cut out eyes and glue them on. Cut a small diamond shape for his beak. Fold this in half and glue on below the eyes, along fold, so his beak 'cheeps'. Glue on 2 small oval-shaped wings.

5. Time for your chick to stand up!
Glue a pair of feet on to the upturned bottle top and stand him on it. Cheep, cheep!

6. Sheep
Paint his body white. Cut an oval shape for his face and glue on to the pointed end of the egg. Cut 2 small ears, 2 eyes and a nose and glue on.

7. Give your sheep a woolly coat and tail
'Paint' his body with glue then cover it with cotton wool balls. Push a small piece of pipecleaner into the hole you made and glue on some cotton wool for his tail.

8. Rabbit
Paint his body brown. Cut out a face and ears and glue on to the body. Glue on 2 eyes, a small nose, and a mouth and some whiskers. Glue on a little cotton wool tail!

Meet the Datestones

Have fun making these pocket-sized people who love to play all day. Pop them in your Super cars (see page 12), or even just in your pocket!

You will need

* Washed datestones
* Coloured acrylic paints
* Paintbrush
* Pipecleaners (cut into 5 cm lengths)
* Modelling clay (for the feet)
* Scraps of wool for hair (you can use plain and paint it after it has dried)
* Multi-purpose clear craft glue
* Safety scissors
* Tissue paper

(see page 12)

What to do

1 **Paint one end of the datestone with flesh-coloured paint** When that is dry choose a colour for the trousers or skirt and paint the other end in this colour.

2 Give your datestone a sweater or T-shirt
Paint a stripe round the middle of the stone.

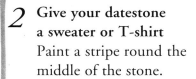

3 Make the legs and feet
Bend the pipecleaner in half and glue it to the back of the datestone. Next make 2 little feet from clay. Push the 2 pipecleaner legs into the "feet", and glue the feet on when the clay has set.

4 Now for the arms and face
Stick a pipecleaner to the back of the stone to make the arms. Paint or draw a face on the flesh-coloured end of the stone.

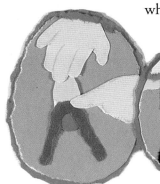
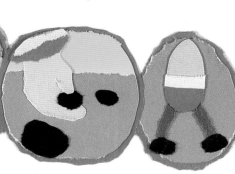

5 Give your tiny person some hair!
Stick small pieces of wool to the head.

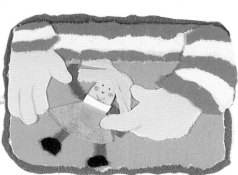

6 If you want to give your datestone a skirt
Wrap a tiny piece of tissue paper round the stone and glue it.

Time for the Datestones to come out and play!

Super cars

All you need is a small box or carton, some coloured straws and a cardboard egg box or a cork. Give your car a Datestone driver and have fun whizzing round the neighbourhood. Watch out for Mr Policestone though!

Don't forget to give your car some lights with the sequins

What to do

1 Make your car
Carefully cut a rectangular-shaped hole out of one side of the box. Paint the box.

2 Now for the wheels
Cut 4 circles from the egg box base. Paint them black. If you are using a cork, ask an adult to cut it into 4 circular slices. Then paint them black.

3 Attach the wheels to your car
Gently, make a hole in each wheel and in the side of the car. Push the paper fastener through the hole in the wheel then the hole in the car. Open out the fastener, so that your wheel is attached.

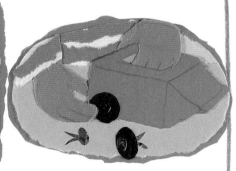

4 Decorate your car with sequins and coloured straws
Cut them into different lengths to fit your car. Or cut them in half for a different effect. Then glue them into place.

5 Time to drive off!
Pop in the sponge for a comfortable seat. Give your car a Datestone driver. Are you ready, Mr Datestone? Drive carefully!

Time for the Datestones to drive off!

Dotty dinosaurs

How many funny names can you think of for your very own collection of unusual dinosaurs – Dottydocus, Stripeysaurus, Starceratops? Have fun printing a Dottydocus with dots or painting a Stripeysaurus with stripes. Stuff them with a little cotton wool and you will find they stand up.

You could make some trees for your dinosaurs to eat, but don't forget to check that they are plant eaters!

What to do

1 **Place the template on a piece of card**
Draw round it, then move your template and draw round it again to make a second shape.

2 **Cut out your 2 dinosaur shapes**
Make a line of glue around the head and down the back to the tip of the tail, on one shape, then stick the other dinosaur shape on top.

3 **Decorate your dinosaur**
Dip the end of a pencil in paint and print a Dottydocus with dots, use a sponge to print a Stripeysaurus with stripes, or decorate a Starceratops with stars. Don't forget to give your dinosaur eyes!

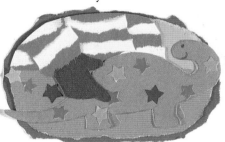

4 **Help your dinosaur stand up**
Tuck a small ball of cotton wool inside his tummy to make him stand up properly.

5 **Make a dinosaur landscape**
Use tubes of rolled-up card for tree-trunks or paint old sweet tubes, and stick on coloured paper leaves.

Put a mermaid princess in your pocket!

Stories are told of a lovely mermaid that lives at the bottom of the sea and sits on a shell throne. Why not make your own beautiful little sea princess to play with. You could keep her in your sea treasure box (see page 18)!

(see page 18)

- Pipecleaner
- Small wooden bead
- Felt for your mermaid's tail
- Scraps of wool for your mermaid's hair
- Small scrap of silver net for tail 'scales'
- Large shell for a 'throne' and 'rockpool'
- Multi-purpose clear craft glue
- Acrylic paints
- Safety scissors
- Pearly beads and small shells for decoration
- Paintbrush
- Silver foil or card for 'rock pool' and mermaid's mirror
- Jewellery wire (for crown)
- Modelling medium for mermaid 'toys'

Jewellery wire threaded with pretty beads makes a lovely mermaid's crown

What to do

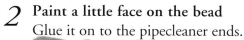

1 Take your pipecleaner and bend it into the shape shown

2 Paint a little face on the bead
Glue it on to the pipecleaner ends.

3 Give your mermaid a tail
Cut out 2 fish tails in felt. Then dot glue on 1 side of each tail shape, and sandwich the long part of the pipecleaner between the 2 tails.

4 Use the scrap of silver net to give her tail some 'scales'
Cut out 2 'tail' shapes in the net and glue them on to the tail.

5 Mermaid's long hair!
Cut several lengths of wool. Tie them together with another piece of wool, knotted across the middle. Glue this to your mermaid's head, and trim to the length you want!

6 Make her a bikini top
Cut 2 small circles from felt, and glue them on. Add a small pearl for decoration.

In stories, mermaids like to sit on rocks and comb their long hair and sing. You could make a beautiful mirror for your mermaid out of silver card or foil with a folded gold or silver sweet paper handle, and decorate it with tiny shells and pearls. Or make her a small comb and 'toys' out of modelling medium.

Fabulous sea picture-pattern treasure boxes

Do you sometimes wish you had a special box to keep all your treasures safe? Now you can make one that everyone will know is yours alone. All you need is a small, empty box or container and some pretty shells and beads, or a few scraps of felt, coloured thread and wool.

You will need

* Small empty boxes or containers
* Pencil
* Paper for sketching
* Acrylic paints
* Paintbrush
* Scraps of felt, coloured thread and wool to make a picture collage OR
* Pretty shells and 'pearly' beads for a mermaid's shell box
* Multi-purpose clear craft glue
* Varnish (for shell box)
* Safety scissors

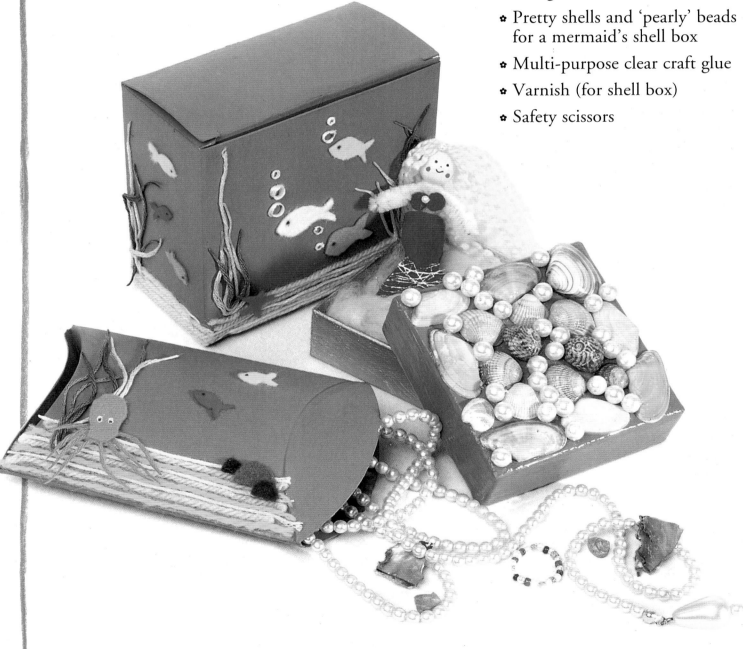

What to do

1 **Mermaid's shell-pattern box**
Plan your design first, making sure that you have enough shells and beads to cover the lid.

2 **Choose a colour for your box and paint it all over, inside and out**
Cover any lettering or pictures. Leave to dry.

3 **Brush each shell or bead with a little craft glue and stick in place**
When dry brush with varnish.

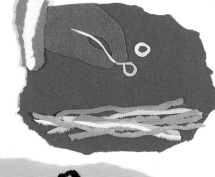

Felt picture collage decoration – what to do

1 **Do a rough sketch of your idea first on paper**
Choose a colour that will be a suitable background colour for your picture and paint your box all over.

2 **Cut out the felt shapes and lengths of thread you need**
Cut out larger shapes first and arrange them. Then cut out smaller shapes and move them around until they feel right.

3 **Different shapes and textures will add variety to your picture**
Here, lengths of wool are used to suggest sand, while fine thread has been used for 'bubbles'.

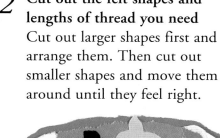
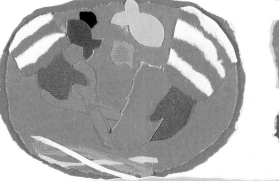
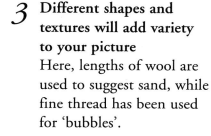

4 **When you are happy with your picture, glue the materials on to the box**
Now your treasure box is ready!

Flying 'sorcerers'

Zip and zoom! Whoosh and swoosh! Make these colourful, magic characters. Watch them fly through the air, with a trail of shining moons and stars sparkling behind them.

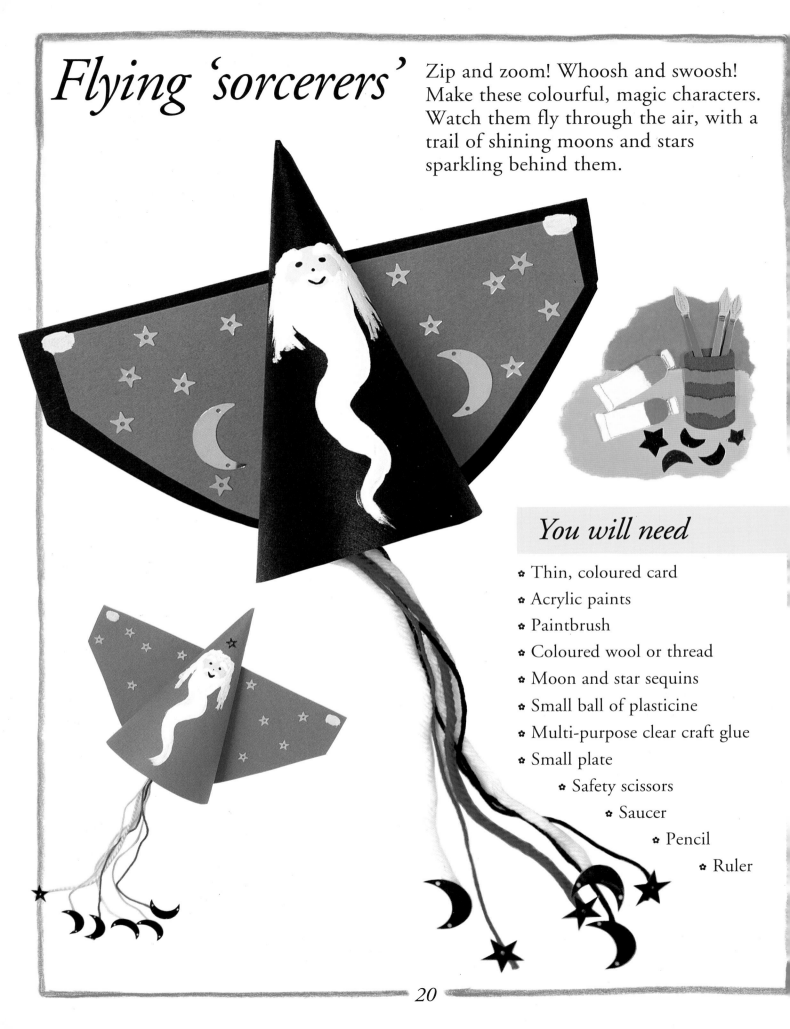

You will need

* Thin, coloured card
* Acrylic paints
* Paintbrush
* Coloured wool or thread
* Moon and star sequins
* Small ball of plasticine
* Multi-purpose clear craft glue
* Small plate
  * Safety scissors
    * Saucer
      * Pencil
        * Ruler

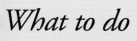

What to do

1 Place the plate on your card and draw round it to make a circle

Using a ruler, divide this in half to make a semi-circle. Cut this shape out.

2 Roll semi-circle shape into a cone

Glue down the overlap to hold the cone in shape.

3 Now for the wings

Take your card again and draw round the saucer. Divide circle in half to make 2 semi-circles. Cut them out and then make a 3rd. Glue all 3 together to form a thicker semi-circle. Make a line of glue down the middle of this and press the cone on to the sticky line.

4 Give your flying 'sorcerer' a face

Paint 2 eyes, a nose and a mouth. If you like give him a long beard and hair.

5 Make him a shining trail

Cut 6 pieces of thread or wool. Knot them together and glue the knotted end inside the cone. Glue your sequins on to the ends.

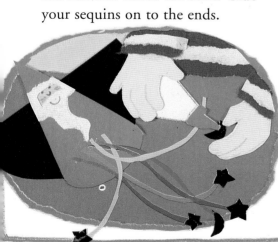

Watch him fly! Push a softened ball of plasticine into the pointed tip of the cone. Whoosh! Off he goes!

Plastic spoon puppets

Have fun collecting plastic spoons in different shapes and sizes and create your own puppet family or a whole zoo of animal puppets.

You will need

- Assorted plastic spoons – small 6 mm spoons make lovely 'baby' puppets, while a round-shaped spoon is just right for an elephant's head!
- Acrylic paints
- Paintbrush
- Books with pictures of wild animals
- Scraps of felt for animal ears, trunks, horns etc
- Scraps of wool for puppet hair, and lace, bits of material and ribbon for clothes and decoration
- Multi-purpose clear craft glue
- Safety scissors

Puppet people – what to do

1 **Paint your spoons flesh-coloured**
Paint all the way down the spoon handle but leave the tip unpainted. When the paint is dry, paint a face on the back of the spoon, with eyes, nose and a mouth.

2 **Give your puppets some 'hair' and 'clothes'**
Glue on small pieces of wool for the hair. Wrap round scraps of material for clothes and glue them to the spoon, then tie a ribbon bow around the 'neck'. A small scrap of lace makes a lovely dress for a 'baby' spoon.

Animal puppets – what to do

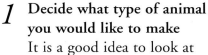

1 **Decide what type of animal you would like to make**
It is a good idea to look at pictures or books to see the special markings that some wild animals have.

2 **Paint the spoon the main colour, for example, orange for a tiger or grey for an elephant**
Look at the picture of your animal again and when the paint is dry add the eyes, nose and mouth.

3 **Give your animals their special markings**
Paint on spots for a giraffe or leopard and stripes for a tiger or zebra.

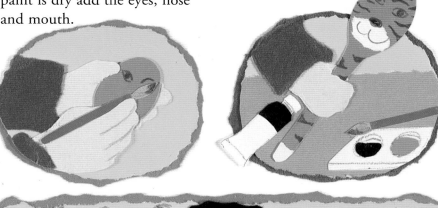

4 **Now for the ears, trunk, or horns**
Cut these out in felt and glue them on to the spoon. Time for your puppets to perform!

Puppet theatre

Make a theatre for your puppets.
All you need is an empty shoebox
and some brightly coloured paints.

You will need

- A shoebox or similar-sized box
- Coloured paper
- Acrylic paints
- Paintbrush
- Safety scissors
- Multi-purpose clear craft glue and brush

What to do

1 **Cut a large window, with shutters in the shoebox**
First draw a rectangle inside the shoebox at one end of the shoebox. Cut along and across the 2 long sides of this rectangle to make your window with shutters.

2 **Paint the box and shutters**
Paint it with stars or stripes in bright colours. Don't forget to paint both sides of the shutters!

3 **Decorate your theatre with shapes to look like drapes**
Using the bright paper, cut out one 'drape' to decorate the top of the theatre and one 'drape' to go along the lower edge of the window. Glue your drapes in place.

Time for the show to start. Everybody ready for opening night?

Unusual mosaic pots

You will need

- Small empty plastic containers
- Plastic bottle (for castle)
- Plastic carton (for castle 'hill') You need one big enough, upturned, for bottle 'castle' to stand on
- Acrylic paints
- Paintbrush
- Old greetings cards
- Safety scissors
- PVA glue and brush
- Multi-purpose clear craft glue

For centuries people have used small pieces of coloured glass or stone to make beautiful patterns and pictures on all sorts of things. These are called mosaics. You can have lots of fun creating beautiful mosaic plant pots or containers by simply cutting up old greetings cards. You can even make a mosaic castle!

Why not make a whole medieval town to play with?

26

What to do

1 **Decide what you want your container to be and then paint it the base colour**
If you are making a castle ask an adult to help you cut the plastic bottle to the right size. Then cut small squares from the top and paint it grey. Paint the carton for your castle 'hill' green.

2 **Carefully cut your cards into small squares**
Think of the pattern you want to make and pick out bright colours to make your pot look really pretty. If you are making your container a castle think about the colours you need to cut, eg – greys for the walls.

3 **When the paint has dried**
Begin to stick the small squares of card on to your pot with the clear glue. Leave tiny gaps between the squares so it looks like a mosaic.

4 **Leave the decorated pot or bottle to dry, then mix some PVA glue with water**
If your pot is to have a plant in it, make 4 holes carefully in the bottom, with the scissors, for drainage.

5 **Brush the glue/water mixture all over the outside of the pot**
Cover the painted part as well as the card pieces. Leave it to dry completely.

6 **Time to fill your pots or bottles!**
Fill them with seed and potting compost and plant your seeds or plants, or fill them with soldiers or pencils!

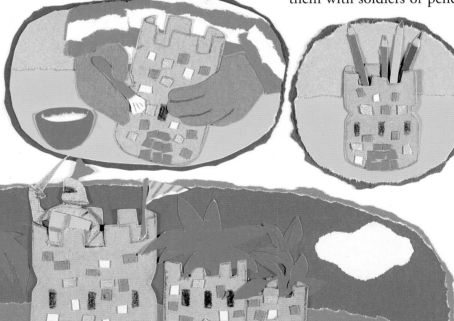

Make a house, fit for a mouse!

Once you have made your house you can decorate it with a variety of home-made and bought accessories and furniture (see p.30)

Have fun making a mouse family complete with their own home. All you need to start off with is a cardboard box, some brazil nuts and paints and paper.

You will need

- Cardboard box
- Small print wrapping paper for wallpaper
- Felt or tile or wood flooring paper cut from magazines
- Felt for mouse ears
- Pencil

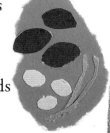

- PVA glue and brush
- Acrylic paints
- Paintbrush
- Brazil nuts
- Wooden beads
- Thick thread

What to do

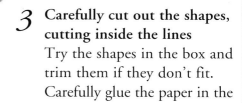

1 Paint the inside top of your box
This will be the 'ceiling' of your mouse house.

2 Decorate the 'walls' of your house with wrapping paper
Place the box on its side on the paper and draw round it. Repeat for the other 2 sides so that you have 3 shapes to cut out.

3 Carefully cut out the shapes, cutting inside the lines
Try the shapes in the box and trim them if they don't fit. Carefully glue the paper in the box, then paint some windows.

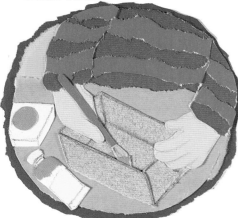

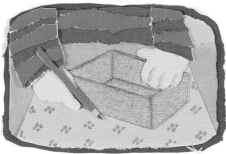

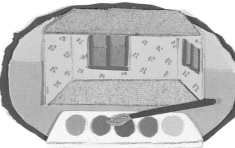

4 Make a floor covering
Cut a piece of felt or plush fabric to make a carpet or cover it with paper to give it a wood or tiled surface.

5 Now for your Mouse Family!
For Mum and Dad, paint the brazil nuts, brown or grey. Use beads for the smaller members of the family. Glue on a thread tail. Then cut out 2 small ears in felt and stick them on.

6 Paint a little face on each mouse and glue on the whiskers
Time for the Mouse family to move in!

Mouse house toys and furniture

Have fun furnishing your mouse house and decorating it with accessories made from a variety of readily available inexpensive things. You could make your mice babies some little toys to play with and a delicious cheese to nibble at when they get hungry. You could even make a broom for the mice parents to sweep up the crumbs with after meals!

Time for tea!

You will need

- ❀ Acrylic paints
- ❀ Pencil
- ❀ Paintbrush
- ❀ Multi-purpose clear craft glue
- ❀ Blu-tack

For a table lamp
- ❀ Toothpaste cap
- ❀ Birthday cake candle-holder
- ❀ Plasticine

For a table
- ❀ Lid of small container
- ❀ A cork
- ❀ Scrap of fabric

For a broom
- ❀ Cocktail stick
- ❀ Dried grasses or straw
- ❀ Short length of thread

For a mirror
- ❀ Silver paper or card or a button
- ❀ Little shells

For wall pictures
- ❀ Stamps, pictures cut out from magazines or buttons and stickers

For a cradle
- ❀ Half a walnut shell
- ❀ Scrap of fabric

For mouse food, plates, toys
- ❀ Modelling clay and varnish (optional)

Curtains
- ❀ 2 pieces of lace, about 5 cm long
- ❀ Cocktail stick, 32 small coloured beads and thread

Flowerpots
- ❀ Cardboard eggbox
- ❀ Small artificial flowers and plasticine

What to do

Table lamp
Paint the cap the colour for the lampshade. Let it dry. Push a small ball of plasticine into the cap. Stand candle-holder upside-down and place cap on it.

Table
Paint cork, then cut a circle of fabric 1 cm bigger than the lid. Glue the cork inside lid, then glue the fabric on to the lid as a tablecloth.

Broom
Cut the dried grasses into 4 cm lengths. Cover 1 end of the cocktail stick with glue and stick the grasses, close together around the stick. Tie a piece of thread tightly round the grasses and glue, then trim the broom if necessary.

Mirror

Cut a piece of silver card to the shape you want and decorate this with a border of shells or gold card, glued to the card. Or use a button as a mirror frame, with foil stuck on for the mirror. Attach your mirror to the wall with blu-tack or double-sided sticking tape.

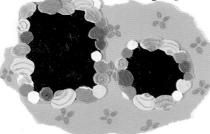

Cheeses

Edam – small ball of modelling clay, with section cut out. When dry, paint outside of ball red, paint cut part, pale yellow. For a cheese with holes, slightly squash ball, put holes in and paint yellow.

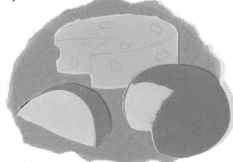

Flower pots

Cut about 1.5 cm off the cone-shaped parts of the eggbox. Paint the pot all over, then push a small ball of plasticine into the bottom of the pot. Arrange the flowers in the pot, pushing them into the plasticine.

Pictures

You can make these from stamps or buttons decorated with small stickers. Or use cut out pictures from magazines and old greetings cards.

Curtains

Push a cocktail stick through the top of both pieces of lace. Thread a bead on each end of the cocktail stick, then tie a piece of thread halfway down the curtain as a tieback. The curtain is held in place with blu-tack.

Mouse toys

Roll several small balls in the clay and shape some into 'building bricks'. Let them dry then paint them in bright colours.

A cradle for the mice babies

Paint the inside of the walnut shell. When dry, tuck a scrap of fabric into the shell for a sheet.

Plates

Take a small piece of modelling clay. Gently mould it round the top of a pencil or large pen. Then squeeze the edges flat. Trim them if too big, remove the pencil and leave the 'plate' to dry. Decorate it with paints or felt tips.